Phoebe Hichens

Dear
Princess

Acknowledgements

Warm thanks to the many schools who helped with this project.

Some were old friends who collaborated with us so wonderfully in our earlier book, *Dear Queen*. Ashford Church of England school, Middlesex; The American schools attached to the USAF base at Upper Heyford; and Bruntsfield Primary school, Edinburgh.

We are also most grateful to our new friends: Brill Church of England Combined School, Aylesbury; Hunter's Tryst School, Edinburgh; Alconbury Elementary School, Huntingdon; St Barnabas Church of England First School, Oxford; Sunnyfields Primary School, London NW4; and The American School in London, NW8.

Children from these schools have contributed enchanting questions and drawings; so once again we must say that without them this book would not have been possible.

Drawings and photographs: The artist for each drawing is given alongside the picture itself – the title page drawing is by Shelly Heim, aged 8. The cover photographs are reproduced by courtesy of Rex Features and the photographs in the colour section are courtesy of Associated Press, Camera Press and Rex Features.

Copyright © 1984 Phoebe Hichens

Designed by Edwin Belchamber

All rights reserved. No reproduction, copy or transmission of this publication may be made without written permission. No paragraph of this publication may be reproduced, copied or transmitted save with written permission or in accordance with the provisions of the Copyright Act 1956 (as amended). Any person who does any unauthorized act in relation to this publication may be liable to criminal prosecution and civil claims for damages.

First published 1984 by
MACMILLAN CHILDREN'S BOOKS
A division of Macmillan Publishers Limited
London and Basingstoke
Associated companies throughout the world

Printed in Hong Kong

ISBN 0 333 37857 1 hardback
ISBN 0 333 37858 X paperback

Preface

It began with the Queen. "Do you ever wear trousers?", "Does your crown wobble?", "Would you rather be shot or poisoned?"

Children from many schools were putting down the questions they would most like to ask the Queen. The result was a book *Dear Queen*. And this proved so popular, it seemed a shame to stop there. Why not go on to the questions they would like to ask a famous and favourite Princess?

Once again, all of us – researchers, teachers, children – had a ball. The questions, the pictures poured in; and it was hard to choose. Sometimes we were tempted to make the book twice as long!

So what we would like to say here is that the children, bless them, have done it again. They have helped create something very special and delightful in the world of royal books.

We'll be dumbfounded if you don't enjoy it.

PHOEBE HICHENS
May 1984

1
First Questions

The Princess of Wales has never been able to conceal her fondness for small, sometimes very small children. And the affection is returned. Four-, five-, six-year-olds love to think they might meet the Princess and ask her questions like these...

Janet, age 4 *"Were you naughty and didn't eat what you was supposed to eat when little girl?"*

The people who helped to bring up Diana remember her as "very sweet natured" and "trying to do the right thing". But she did, of course, have likes and dislikes. One nanny, Miss Thompson, told her she must eat the crusts on her bread – not just pull them off and leave them. For a time it looked as if little Diana was obeying. But then Miss Thompson discovered a pile of crusts under the nursery table.

Kerry, age 6 *"Do you wear tights or not?"*

Hard to imagine the Queen going around with bare legs. One little boy even thought the Queen Mum 'went to bed in long johns, thermal'. But Diana had a more relaxed upbringing than other members of the Royal Family. She still likes to be comfortable as well as smart; and in hot weather, she has been photographed wearing neither stockings nor tights.

Flora Holmes, age 7 *"Did you go to playschool?"*

Yes. She went to a nursery school in King's Lynn.

Daniel Blomfield, age 6 *"Do you like playing chess? I like playing chess."*

Daniel must be a clever fellow. Not many children of six play chess – and Diana didn't. She adored dressing-up games, like charades, which weren't so brainy. She still does; and this is lucky because charades are a favourite game of the Royal Family. (Mark Phillips doesn't like them at all!)

Do you like shaking different people's hands?

– Alex

Alex, age 7 *"Do you like shaking different people's hands?"*

A small boy in a crowd once managed to get a word with the Princess. He said: "She told me, 'Please don't squeeze my hand too tight. After lots of squeezes, it starts to hurt.' " On another occasion a man held her hand for so long, she had to say: "Please can I have it back?" Shaking hundreds of hands can be hard work; and the Princess is likely to go on begging: "Not too many squeezes!" After a tiring session she soaks her hands in iced water – a tip from Prince Charles.

Jeremy Jones, age 7 *"What do you do with your presents?"*

Depends on the present. Sedgemoor Council decided to give the royal couple a very practical wedding gift: a ton of peat. That went on their garden at Highgrove. Other presents included lots of cakes, made by children, and decorated with smarties, chocolate drops, sugar mice and pictures of Prince Charles. Diana thought they were lovely but couldn't eat them all. Many were given away to children in hospital. Gifts from family and friends are kept and loved – just as you and I keep our presents.

Emma, age 6 *"What is your second name and third name and why do you have them?"*

Diana's second name is Frances, after her mother. She doesn't have a third one. As for Diana: that just seems to have been a name her parents liked. No special reason.

Johnnie, age 4 *"Would you like to have been a little boy instead of a little girl?"*

Little girls can be tomboys; and it's said that Princess Anne went through a stage of wanting to be a boy. But Diana always loved dolls and cuddly toys and babies and cooking and party frocks. She enjoyed being a girl – and still does.

Isobel, age 5 *"What makes you cry?"*

Soon after they became engaged, Prince Charles went off on a tour of Australia, New Zealand, Venezuela and America. He was to be gone for five weeks, which must have seemed a terribly long time. When they said goodbye, Diana couldn't hold back her tears. Probably she'll never be like the Queen who, even as a child, was not seen to cry in public.

Neddy, age 5 *"Do they make you tidy things up?"*

Like the Queen, Diana has always been a tidy person. Nobody has had to nag her much about this. Charles, on the other hand, is not a bit tidy. He leaves piles of things lying about, hates throwing anything away, is always going "to sort it all out" but seldom does.

Edie, age 4 *"Did you feel funny when you met the Queen?"*

No – because she was too little to know the Queen *was* the Queen. Diana grew up on the Sandringham estate, next door to the home of the Royal Family. She can never remember a time when she didn't know them. In her earliest memories, the Queen was someone called "Aunt Lilibet".

Jane, age 5 *"Do you get the giggles when you shouldn't have?"*

She got the giggles whispering with Charles when the National Anthem was being played. The Queen thought she shouldn't have and gave the pair a pretty frosty look. (But it's happened to the Queen, too. She got helpless giggles once, watching some African dancers.)

Jen, age 6 *"What do you think of Prince Andrew? Is he a bit rough?"*

As a boy, he was quite a bit rougher and tougher than Prince Charles. "Andrew, *don't* do that!" was often said – by both parents. But he and Diana were good friends. She says: "Andrew and I used to gang up together." And as a schoolgirl, she would write to him, not Charles. This was natural for Andrew was only a year older. She will always remember him as a good childhood friend.

Louise, age 7 *"Were you jellus when you had a little brother? I was."*

It's quite usual for the youngest member of the family to feel jealous when another baby comes along. And in the Spencer family, the little brother following Diana was likely to be a special pet. The only other baby boy had died and this was the longed-for son and heir. But even at three years old, Diana felt very loving and motherly towards the newcomer. She was only cross if anyone stopped her playing with him.

Jennifer Clark 11

Tommy, age 6 *"Have you lots of blue blood?"*

Yes, lots. The Spencer family are related to most of the British Monarchs. And she can even go one better than Prince Charles for she is a direct descendant of Charles I and Charles II and he is not. Both the Prince and Princess of Wales can trace their ancestors back to the Great Kings of Parthia who reigned in Persia and Babylonia over two thousand years ago.

Tim Heston, age 7 *"Did you run away from school?"*

Not exactly. But when Diana was sent to a finishing school in Switzerland, she became terribly homesick. She missed her friends and her family. She couldn't get used to living outside Britain. After six weeks, she asked to leave.

Mary, age 7 *"Did you like your daddy? I like my daddy but he doesn't live at home any more."*

She was lucky in so many ways. But there was one misfortune she had to share with millions of other children. Diana was only six years old when, suddenly, her mother didn't live at home any more. Suddenly, there were two families instead of one. It was bound to be strange and sad. And to this day, the Princess would understand only too well how seven-year-old Mary must feel.

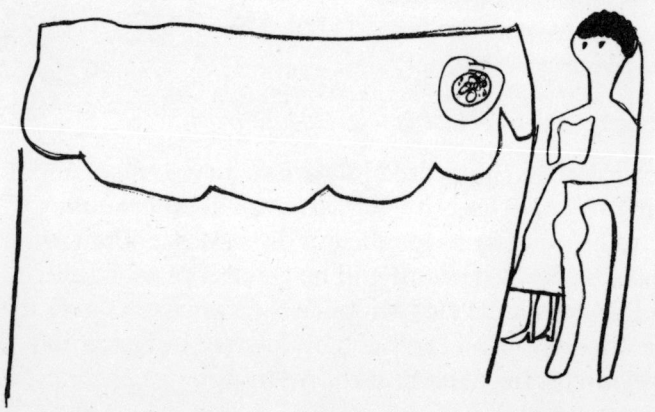

Dear Princess Diana do you have nice or mean gests? Christopher Samuel age 7

2
The Most Asked Questions of All

It probably won't surprise you to hear that questions on royal babies came up again and again and again. Often they were the same questions – or very nearly.

So we have divided this section into two parts: there are the most-asked general questions and then there are the most-asked "royal baby" questions.

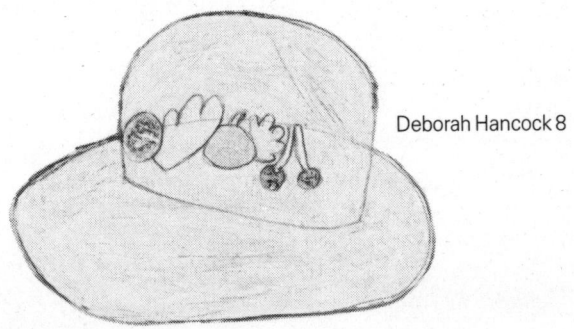

Deborah Hancock 8

"Who makes your hats?"

She might buy a hard riding hat from Locke's in St James's. But when it comes to something gorgeous and fashionable to go with her newest dress or coat – there's only one hatter in the Princess's life. That hatter is a Scotsman, John Boyd. It was Diana's mother, Mrs Shand Kydd, who brought the two together during the hectic, pre-wedding shopping spree; and Diana was so enchanted with his designs she has been faithful to him ever since. He thinks she has the most wonderful head to put things on and only complains that everything is wanted in such a hurry. Sometimes he is only handed a belt or a scrap of material to show him what the outfit to go under his newest hat will be like. "But she's such a *nice* wee girl," he says. "So polite."

Martin Tate 11

"Do you like living in a palace?"

She doesn't spend much time living in a real palace. For a real palace is the official residence of the reigning Monarch; and in Britain that means Buckingham Palace, Windsor Castle and Holyroodhouse. The Prince and Princess of Wales do have the use of a flat in Windsor Castle; but home is divided between Highgrove House (their house in Gloucestershire) and an apartment on three floors in Kensington Palace. They wouldn't call either of them *real* palaces.

Dear Princess Diana
What do you like best about Buckigham Palace?
CAitlin Hurcombe
age 5

"Do you have a four-poster bed?"

Yes. Prince Charles has always liked them. (He had one for many years in his rooms at Buckingham Palace.) The Princess likes them, too.

"Did you have a nickname at school?"

It's said that she was called Duchess. Some of her schoolfellows remember her as being "quite dignified". She may even have been a bit prim. Certainly sounds rather a heavy nickname for a pretty young girl.

"Who does your hair?"

Kevin Shanley of the Chelsea studio, Head Lines. Other hairdressers have grumbled: "He didn't really create a new hairstyle... the Lady Di look was quite old-fashioned..." But who cares? The Lady Di look became one of the most famous, most imitated hairstyles in the world. At first Kevin was concerned to suit her face, her colouring. But now he follows her round the world wondering: "How will the hair look under this hat? that tiara? burning sun? pouring rain?" It's quite a problem keeping ahead with a travelling, trend-setting Princess; and most people think he does a spectacular job.

"What're your favourite sports?"

Swimming. Skiing. Fishing.

"Can you afford anything you want?"

Diana doesn't think so. When she and Prince Charles gave their first dinner party, it's said that the chef recommended lobster. Diana said: "Can we afford it?"

"Are you good at being on time?"

Yes. Like her tidiness, punctuality is one of her virtues. And it's not one shared by all members of the Royal Family. It's said that the Queen Mother was only early once in her life – and that was when she was born. Her mother didn't manage to get to the hospital on time and the baby was born in the ambulance.

Danielle Chaput 9

"What books do you read?"

She enjoyed the romances of her step-grandmother, Barbara Cartland. Well, she would, wouldn't she? The pure and beautiful young heroine always marries the marvellous and mature hero!

Omar 7

"Do your family like horses the way the Royal Family do?"

Many of her family certainly did. One Earl Spencer was a great hunter. It was said that he ran the Pytchley Hunt "like a regiment of dragoons". And when the Empress Elizabeth of Austria came to visit, a messenger, bringing news of the death of the Pope, was told to keep quiet until the day's hunting was over. Her Apostolic Majesty, the Earl insisted, would not want to be interrupted while pursuing the fox.

Diana herself is not so keen. A bad fall and a broken arm turned her against horses. She continues to ride, but not with the enthusiasm of the Queen or Princess Anne.

Michelle Stathman 10

"Where do you get your clothes?"

Before her engagement, Diana browsed happily round many London shops, specially those in Knightsbridge. But those days are over. Now she goes to famous designers like Belinda Belville and David Sassoon. (Known as the Belville Sassoon partnership.) They are favourites of Princess Alexandra and the Duchess of Kent too. She also goes to designers Jean Muir, Bill Paisley and, of course, David and Elizabeth Emmanuel who made her wedding dress. Again, it was her mother, Mrs Shand Kydd, who first took her to all these glamorous salons and helped her choose. She is always on the look-out for new talent and recently discovered a Japanese designer, Hachi, who she likes very much. He made the dress glittering with crystal beads which was such a success in Australia.

"What's your favourite piece of jewellery?"

She's bound to think back to the evening of February 22nd 1980 when she dined with the Queen at Windsor Castle. It was just over two weeks since Prince Charles had proposed and the engagement was still a family secret. After dinner, a dazzling tray of rings from the Royal Jewellers, Garrards, was brought in. Diana was told to choose. She picked out a diamond and sapphire ring; and when this had been slipped on her finger by the Prince, she felt truly "engaged". A magic moment. To this day, the Queen wears the ring given to her by Lieutenant Philip Mountbatten. Thirty, forty, fifty years from now, we can be pretty sure the diamond and sapphire gem will still be on Diana's finger.

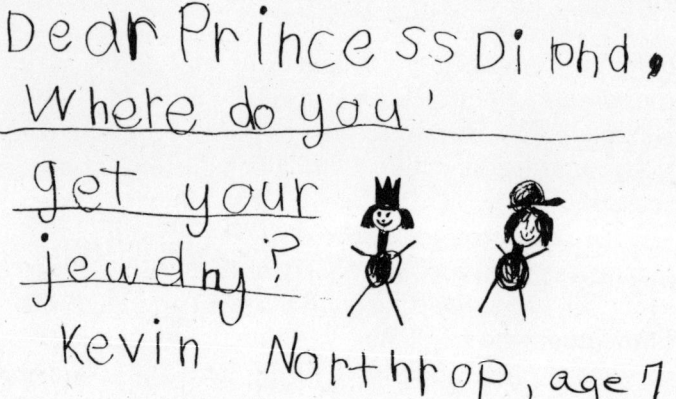

Dear Princess Diana,
Where do you get your jewdry?
Kevin Northrop, age 7

"Can you do the ironing?"

Yes. As a teenager she even used to iron drip-dry items, like blue jeans. It may not have been strictly necessary; but when it comes to clothes, the Princess has always been a perfectionist.

"Did you like school?"

She may not have cared much for the uniform at her preparatory school, Riddlesworth Hall near Diss. Grey shorts, maroon jersies and hair worn off the collar. Not much fun for a girl who loved pretty clothes. But then she moved on to West Heath near Sevenoaks. This is quite a grand school (fees of over £4,000 a year now for boarders) with lacrosse and hockey fields, a heated swimming pool and eight tennis courts. As well as the usual subjects, girls can learn ballet, tap dancing, pottery and playing the drum. Diana enjoyed the dancing and swimming more than the Latin and Physics. There was no formal uniform and she was glad to get out of the grey shorts, too!

"Do you cook for Prince Charles?"

She has taken a Cordon Bleu Cookery Course; and, when sharing a London flat with friends, she enjoyed taking turns in the kitchen. But as Princess of Wales, there isn't much time for cooking. She *could* still produce a family meal, and this is more than the Queen could manage. As a child Princess Elizabeth had little experience in cooking.

"What's your favourite colour?"

As a bachelor girl, she could be into strong and dashing colour schemes. The bathroom in her London flat had a vivid cherry wallpaper. The sitting room was decorated in a yellow which one friend described as "a bit overpowering". Now she goes for softer shades. Sunshine yellow remains a favourite, but toned down to a *gentle*, almost cloudy effect.

"Do you get sick of photographers?"

Yes. Particularly when she considers herself "off duty". On an official engagement, she knows the cameras have to be there. But one can't blame her for wanting to keep private holidays, swimming or skiing out of range. On occasions she has flatly refused to be photographed.

"Have Princesses of Wales been good mothers or bad?"

Some of them didn't have much chance to be either. In the early days, royal mothers saw little of their children because the court was always on the move and the babies did not travel around with the parents. They would be left with foster parents and guardians.

The first Princess of Wales was Joan, wife of the Black Prince (son of Edward III) and known as the Fair Maid of Kent. They had two children; but Joan was said to be more interested in parties and pleasure than mothering. A later princess, wife of the future George IV, was on such bad terms with her husband, she was allowed little contact with Princess Charlotte, their only child.

Perhaps the first really warm and caring mother was Princess Alexandra, wife of Edward VII. All her children adored her. But Princess May, later Queen Mary and grandmother of the present Queen, was said to be aloof. Certainly she failed to notice that her two eldest little boys were badly bullied by a cruel nanny. The present Princess of Wales looks like being the ideal mother; but she is helped by modern life which assumes all parents – even busy, royal ones who travel a lot – will have a close and loving relationship with their children.

"How tall are you?"

Five feet ten inches – almost exactly the same height as Prince Charles.

Tressa Hamm 8

"What do you measure?"

When she's not expecting a baby, the Princess takes a size ten. She measures twenty-two inches round the waist.

Caroline Aroe 7

"What's your favourite food?"

She loves yoghourt. But in earlier days it's said that her top favourite – shared with so many other children – was baked beans.

"Do all your family like clothes?"

Her mother does and has had a lot of influence on the leader-of-fashion Princess. And both her elder sisters, Lady Jane and Lady Sarah, worked for *Vogue* before they were married.

"Did you make many friends at school? Do you have a best friend?"

Her closest friend has probably been Carolyn Pride. They met at West Heath; and later Carolyn was to be one of her flatmates in London. The Princess remains faithful to her old friends many of whom date from her schooldays. When the engagement had been announced, and a royal car arrived to take her to Clarence House as the guest of the Queen Mother – her last words to her three flatmates were: "Please telephone me. I'm going to need you!"

"Do you ever put your foot down?"

Although Diana, ever since childhood, has been described as "sweet natured", it's been added that she is "no pushover". So the answer is yes: sometimes her foot does come down. One example was her decision to take young William on their visit to Australia. Even the loving parents, George VI and Queen Elizabeth, never took their little daughters with them when they went abroad. (And sometimes these tours lasted many months.) There were also a lot of "do's" and "don'ts" about royal travel. Less than forty years ago there was a long argument in Parliament: "should Princess Elizabeth, heir to the throne, *fly the Atlantic?* Was this not far too dangerous?" When flying became an accepted part of the royal lifestyle, there were still taboos on members of the Royal Family flying in the same plane. Supposing it crashed? But the Princess took a firm line. For the first time, the baby came too. What's more, they all went in the same plane.

> Dear Princess Diana,
> Do you do exercises?
> Does Prince William do exercises?
> Does Prince Charles do exercises?
>
> Laili Khalat Bari 8

"Are you into aerobic exercises?"

She loves exercises done to music; but she has noticed the warnings that aerobics can be *too* energetic: can, in fact, damage the body. So she keeps to the safer exercises – many of them learnt when she was hoping to be a ballet dancer.

"What kind of sheets do you have?"

All white. All in pure Irish linen. They need ironing, which would be a big chore for most of us; but the Princess has enough help in the house to cope with the work.

"Did you mind having a stepmother?"

Most children do, especially if their own mother is still alive and much loved. The Spencer children did find it difficult to accept their father's new wife, Raine. But by then, Diana was fourteen. Her parents had been separated for eight years: she was old enough to understand his need for a companion. She came to admire her stepmother's enormous energy and the way she turned the family home at Althorp into a very successful business. More than anything, she admired her determination not to let the Earl die when he suffered a terrible brain haemorrhage. Many doctors thought he couldn't possibly live. Raine refused to believe them. In the end she was proved right; and her stepchildren agree that she almost certainly saved his life.

"Did you think you would be a princess when you were little?"

Yes, of course. Living so close to three Princes – what girl wouldn't?

"What would you like to be if you weren't a princess?"

Her dream was to be a ballet dancer. But even if she hadn't married Prince Charles, this dream could not have come true. She grew to be too tall.

Dear Princess Diana,
What do you do at home?
Do you like being a princess?

Julie Vetter, 9

Royal Baby Questions

"Is Prince William good, bad or just average?"

He's not a goody-good boy. Has even been described as "quite a handful". He's active and inquisitive and gets into forbidden things – like the burglar alarm

Aimée Phillips 6

system at Kensington Palace which he managed to set off. He's been known to stick out his tongue at photographers. And it's said he likes to throw his bootees down the loo. And not only his own boots either. An expensive pair of shoes, belonging to his father, went the same way. All in all, he's pretty normal!

"Who looks after Prince William when you go out?"

There's a full-time nanny and under-nanny. But it's known that Diana regrets the amount of time she has to spend away from her son. In Australia she met a housewife with a bawling fifteen-month-old baby. The Australian said: "I wish I had a nanny to look after my baby like you have. It must be marvellous to go off and relax sometimes." But Diana looked surprised. "Oh, I'd swap places with you any time. I'd much rather have William with me than leave him behind with his nanny."

"What's it like where Prince William lives?"

Highgrove House, the Gloucestershire home, has four reception rooms, nine bedrooms, five dressing rooms, six bathrooms, a nursery wing and a servants' wing. The Princess likes pinkish pastel shades for the nursery as well as for her own bedroom. The same light colour schemes surround the little Prince at Kensington Palace. Here the family live on three floors: nursery, nanny's quarters, night nursery on the top floor. There is also a barbecue on the roof and a helicopter pad in the garden. One can see Prince William getting interested in both of those!

"What does Prince William call his daddy?"

Just that. "Daddy." And it's unusual because traditionally royal children – including Charles – call their fathers "Papa".

Sarah Davey 11

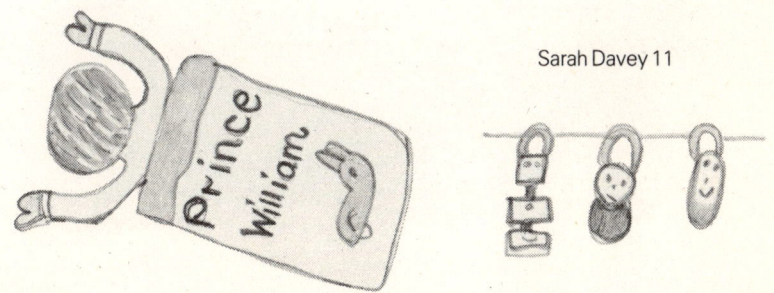

"Does Peter Phillips play with his mummy and daddy?"

Yes, he does. Whenever possible there are nursery teas and games with both parents. Young Peter specially likes wrestling matches with his father and reading aloud with his mother. There are, of course, the riding lessons. And though Mark Phillips admits, "I don't spend nearly as much time with Peter as I would like," he goes on to say that on a free afternoon when he ought to be doing dozens of other things "... I'll spend the time with him. If I'm in the workshop mending something and he wants to hold a spanner or pass the hammer, it all takes much longer because you have to watch everything and make sure it's safe. But at least he's helping Papa."

"Does Prince William like chocolate?"

No, not specially. He takes after his father who has never been very keen on the taste.

Mark Rose 8

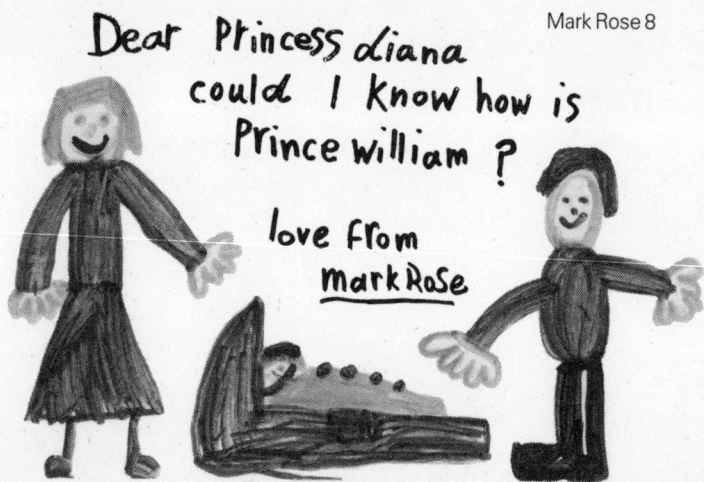

"Does Prince William have a lot of money?"

Not yet. But when he comes to inherit the Duchy of Cornwall from Prince Charles it's thought that his assets will run into billions. At the moment income from the Duchy is around £770,000 a year.

Eleanor Churchlow 4½

"Is anyone allowed to smack royal babies?"

Many royal children have been beaten very hard. The sons of George III were "flogged like dogs" by the footmen. And Prince Albert, husband of Queen Victoria, frequently beat his eldest son, Edward. The young Prince was not clever at his lessons, and his father would punish him severely. But, as with other families, much depends on the parents. George and Elizabeth, parents of the present Queen, were very gentle. Prince Philip was stricter; but most friends reckon that the Prince and Princess of Wales won't go in for more than the gentlest cuff.

Ruth 10

"Which babies are royal?"

Depends what you mean by "royal". A lot of babies can claim to have "royal blood". If one goes back far enough, it's believed that most British families have some connection with royalty. The number of Edward I's descendants runs into millions. But if you ask: "Which baby has the right to the title *Royal Highness*?" – the answer is "not very many". All children of the monarch are Royal Highnesses. So are the children of the monarch's sons. But there's sex discrimination here. The children of the daughters – the children, for instance, of Princess Margaret or Princess Anne – cannot claim the title. Princess Anne's children are simply "Master Peter" and "Miss Zara". Princess Margaret's children are Viscount Linley and Lady Sarah only because their father – unlike Mark Phillips – accepted a title. Any babies, however, of Prince Andrew and Prince Edward will be royal princes and princesses. After that, it "dies out". The grandchildren of Prince Andrew may have no title at all – certainly not Royal Highness. Got it?

"Do doctors who have royal babies get a lot of money?"

Mr George Pinker, who delivered Prince William, wouldn't dream of saying whether or not he had had a royal bonus for the royal birth. But we do know that, in earlier days, a well-pleased royal father could be generous. When James II knew that his wife had had a son, he immediately knighted the doctor and gave the midwife five hundred guineas "to buy herself some breakfast".

"Does William have pictures in his room?"

Yes. At Highgrove House, the day nursery is said to be covered with a wonderland of animals and picturebook characters.

"Do you make your babies eat things that are good for them, like bran?"

The Princess is a great believer in healthy foods like bran. If her children don't grow up to be pictures of health – "splendid physical specimens" as Earl Spencer described his own daughters – it won't be her fault.

"Does William like trains?"

Too early to say for sure. But it looks as if he may have a special reason for enjoying train rides in the future. A special nursery carriage was once designed for Prince Charles and Princess Anne. This was attached to the Royal Train so that the youngsters could travel with their parents – but in their own quarters. One of the features was large cupboards to store lots of games and cuddly animals and other toys. We all know that the Prince and Princess of Wales like the family to stay together and travel together as much as possible; so it's thought that, pretty soon, the special toys and nursery furniture will be brought out of storage, the nursery coach dusted down and put back in service – and who knows, we may see it passing through our local station.

Nichola Ancill 10

Jason Rossi 10

Diana looked good in a hat – even then
With one of the few horses she really liked

...oming down the steps of ...Paul's after the most ...evised wedding in the ...orld

...etting ready for the ...edding: an informal ...cture by the Queen's ...usin, Lord Lichfield

The Princess in her element with lots of children. Australia, 1983

an you see another royal rubbing noses with such charm? New Zealand, 1983

The mother who refused to leave her baby behind. New Zealand, 1983

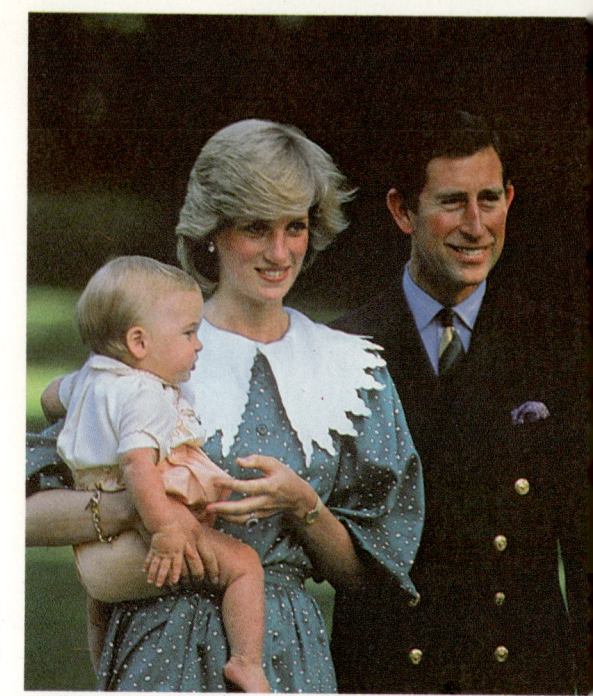

First photographed toddle-about in Kensington Palace: eighteen-month-old Prince William with proud parents

e of the most asked questions from children: "Where do you get your hats?"

Charlotte Brown 8

Zoë Matthews 10

When you have another baby what would you call it and will it have lots of names?

Yours sincerley
Hazel Tucker.

"Do you give Prince William his bath?"

Yes – on the nanny's night out. Prince Charles joins in whenever possible, and it's a great treat for all three. They're not the first royal parents to enjoy bathtime. As Duke and Duchess of York, George and Elizabeth would be up most evenings to supervise the little princesses, Elizabeth and Margaret Rose, splashing around. Later, there would be pillow fights in the bedroom. "Please don't get the children too excited!" the nanny, Alah, would beg. But sometimes, no one listened to her.

"Does Prince Charles call William anything except William?"

When the name was chosen, it was said firmly that there were to be no "shortenings". No Willies or Billies. But it seems that Prince Charles has not quite kept to this. He usually calls his young son "Wills".

Gillian Russell 11

Prince Charles
Would you like a girl this time?

3
Funny Questions

There have been the questions we expected. But round the corner there has always been something marvellously *un*expected. Here are some of our surprises.

Martin Pridie *"Would you like to have quads and get it over with?"*

Definitely not. Diana has said that four, five or six babies – all coming together – would be *too much*. Even one at a time has its drawbacks (like morning sickness). But she does admit that "the end product is worth it".

Millie *"Have you ridden elephants and other things?"*

She's ridden a camel and found it bumpy. So has Prince Charles who once took part in a camel race and said: "I was petrified."

Wot car have you got?
Best Wishes from Russell. 8.

Russell Holloway

Doreen Chapel *"Do you go on dancing much before your babies is born?"*

Maybe. But not in public. Queen Charlotte, wife of George III, might have found this surprising. She herself danced the night away with the French Ambassador at a palace ball only hours before her eighth child was born.

Deborah Hancock 8

Deborah *"Is Prince Charles scared of Jaws?"*

Probably. Who isn't?

Mary and Carol *"What's the most awful thing that ever happened to you?"*

Diana still remembers with dismay a famous "see through" photograph. It was before the announcement of her engagement, and Fleet Street reporters managed to position her in bright sunlight. The camera showed up the fact that she was wearing no slip under her skirt. Poor Diana exclaimed: "I don't want to be remembered as the girl who didn't wear a petticoat!"

Maurice Trotter *"Did Charles sit with you when you had the baby and say mind it's a boy?"*

Prince Charles did sit with her. He said afterwards that at times all he could think was: "Oh, you poor thing. What have I let you in for?" But no doubt he was pleased to find it was a boy because the Royal Family like to begin with a son and heir. When Queen Victoria had her first child, the doctor almost apologised. "Oh Madam, it is a Princess!" And the Queen didn't pretend to be very pleased, either. "Next time it will be a Prince," she said firmly. (And it was.)

Daniel Ayton 7

Daniel *"Do you like the pound coin?"*

She won't have to think about it much because Royalty hardly ever handle notes or coins. The Princess puts money into the collection plate at Church, but that will probably be a five pound note. In due course, Prince William may be handed a pound coin by his parents when he goes to Church with them. (The young princesses, Elizabeth and Margaret, were given a shilling.) No reason otherwise why Diana and the pound coin should ever meet up.

Samantha Hinton 9

Denys *"Could you have married Charles if you hadn't been a Lady?"*

Diana lived next door to the Royal Family, was indeed a relation, belonged in their circle ... of course this helped. Not every girl can expect to meet a Prince, let alone marry him. But the rules about royal marriages have certainly been changed. In an interview, some years before his marriage, Prince Charles made it clear that he didn't *have* to marry a royal or titled lady. It was a question of finding someone who could cope with the life, with the job. This was his great worry when he fell in love with Diana. Did she know what she was letting herself in for?

Gilly *"Do you like cartoons?"*

It's said she has quite a collection in a downstairs lavatory at Kensington Palace. They all make fun of Prince Charles.

Michelle Hawes 9

Lola Jones *"Do you think Prince Charles ought to wear snazzier clothes?"*

Possibly. But not *too* snazzy. She has persuaded him to wear slip-on shoes instead of the conservative lace-ups. He has even been coaxed into striped shirts, bolder ties, colourful sweaters and double-breasted suits. It's not wildly adventurous. But Diana can see that conventional clothes really suit him, and that few people want a Prince of Wales dressed like Screaming Lord Sutch.

Nick Barns *"Do you have to make do with a secondhand Crown until you become a proper Queen?"*

There are four Royal Crowns. The Crown of St Edward which is only used at the Coronation, the Imperial State Crown, worn at important state occasions – like the Opening of Parliament – the Imperial Crown of India, made for George V when he visited India (it had to be made specially because he wasn't allowed to take any of the other Crowns out of Britain), and the Consort Crown, made for the Queen Mother in 1937. As Princess of Wales, Diana is not entitled to wear any of these Crowns. She will have to wait until Charles becomes King before she can wear the Consort Crown: the only one of the four that will ever be hers by right. Beautiful tiaras from the collection of royal jewellery are not official Crowns. She can wear these at any time.

Kelly-Jane Burgess 10

Dear Priness Diana and Prince Charles,

Please will you tell me about the very first animals you ever had, Perhaps hamsters like mine?

your faithful friend,
Kelly-Jane Burgess.

> Dear Lady Diana Do you like tarantulas?

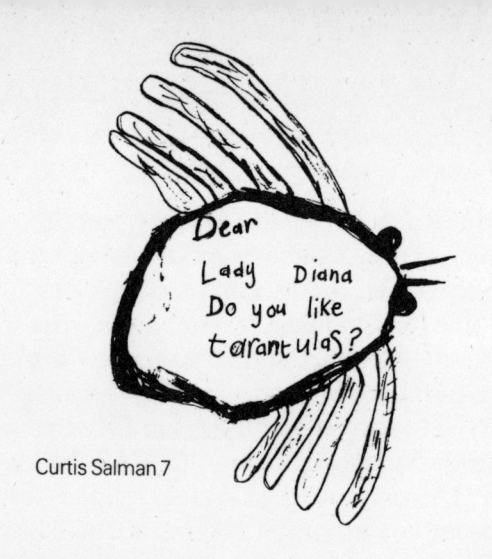

Curtis Salman 7

Charlotte, age 7 *"Have you ever holded a tarantula?"*

No. She doesn't plan to, either.

Susie *"Can Prince Charles sew?"*

He doesn't have much talent with the needle; but his grandfather, George VI, did. He once made a dozen chair covers in petit point.

Heather *"Would I earn more than the miners if I was a royal nanny?"*

Barbara Barnes, nanny to Prince William, only earns about £80 a week. On the other hand, she gets free food, some free travel, generous holidays and a very nice place to live in.

Hebe *"What would you like Charles to be if he wasn't a Prince?"*

When the question was put to a mutual friend of the royal couple, she laughed and said: "Probably a dress designer."

Keith Turner *"Do you laugh when Prince Charles falls off his horse?"*

She looks terrified. Riding accidents can hurt people very badly; and when Edward VIII was Prince of Wales, the Prime Minister asked him to give up steeplechasing. The possible "falls" were just too dangerous.

Paul Mortyn-Jones *"Do you like greasy chips?"*

No, not much.

Don *"Did they put a 'Just Married' sign on the gold coach?"*

Not on the gold coach, which is used for coronations. But Prince Andrew tied silver and blue gas balloons and a "Just Married" sign to the carriage which took the Prince and Princess of Wales off on their honeymoon.

Samantha Elms 8

Dear Princess Diana
How many coachs have you been in?
and do you like it in the coachs?
love from Samantha Elms.

Lucy *"Does the Prime Minister help you have your babies?"*

Prime Ministers have never "helped". Not like midwives or doctors. But at one time it was the custom for them to be present at a royal birth. Reliable witnesses were thought to be needed because a queen – desperate to produce an heir to the throne – might fake the whole thing and try to pass off someone else's baby as her own. The ritual was still going on in the time of the present Queen's great-great-grandmother. When Victoria went into labour with her first child, the Prime Minister, the Foreign Secretary, the Lord Chancellor, the Archbishop of Canterbury, the Bishop of London and the Comptroller of the Royal Household were hastily summoned. (They can't have been very pleased because this was at four-thirty in the morning of a bitter November day.) The Queen refused to have them at her bedside "to view our discomfort" so they waited next door. When the baby was born, they trooped in to inspect. They probably felt it was all a bit ridiculous, and the custom has since been dropped. No question of Mrs Thatcher or Sir Geoffrey Howe hanging around St Mary's Hospital, Paddington when a new royal baby is due.

Angus *"What do you think about kilts?"*

She thinks they suit Prince Charles, but they're not a great favourite of hers. Queen Victoria – who was thrifty about children's clothes – liked kilts because they could be handed down to younger daughters as well as younger sons. Diana is unlikely to think this is much of a plus.

Edwin *"Did you think the train on your wedding dress was too long?"*

It took a lot of managing. But the Princess practised with a long sheet pinned to her shoulders. Other royal brides have gone through the same drill.

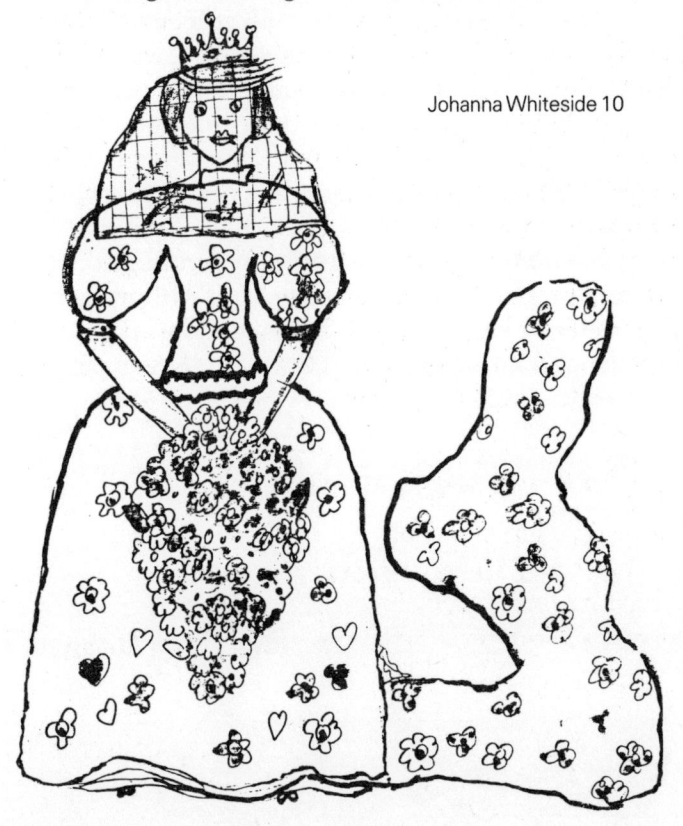

Johanna Whiteside 10

Charles *"Why do you want to be so thin?"*

Same reason many other girls would give. She likes the clothes that look good on a slim figure.

Lettice *"Did you tell Prince Charles you would marry him before he asked you?"*

"I was amazed she took me on," said Prince Charles. "I never had any doubts about it," said Lady Diana. And although nineteen-year-old girls don't go around proposing to the Heir to the Throne, it seems that the Princess knew her own mind more clearly than the Prince. Perhaps it runs in the family. The third Earl Spencer, before he had inherited the title and was still Viscount Althorp, met a lady ten years younger than himself. In those days, the lady was *very definitely* not supposed to make the first moves, and the biographer wrote solemnly: "Having become on very slight acquaintance deeply interested in Lord Althorp, she contrived to let him know it." This was, he added, a very dangerous experiment. However, they married and lived happily ever after.

Simon 6

Dear princess Diana

Do you like mices?

love from Simon

4
Questions From Round The World

We don't pretend to have travelled all round the world in order to get these questions. But we did try to find schools in Britain with children from many other countries. And we were lucky. We found the children; and many of the questions were lovely.

Bruce, from Australia *"Do you think Prince William looks like the Queen or your daddy?"*

Quite a few friends have said young William looks like Earl Spencer. Same round face. And this may not be anything to do with it – but the grandfather very much admires the Prince. When he first saw him, aged only a day, he said he was such a nice, smooth-faced baby. Not all wrinkled and crunched up, the way many infants are.

Joan, from Australia *"What did you like best about Australia?"*

It was her first big tour abroad as Princess of Wales and she loved the friendliness of the people. She found them warm and welcoming and very interested in Prince William: a sure way to any young mother's heart.

Donald Kitzmiller, from Maryland USA *"What's your favourite country?"*

The Princess has done a fair bit of travelling since her marriage, but nowhere near as much as the Queen or Prince Philip or her husband. She'd like to see more of the world before answering such a question.

Keya 8

Keya, 8, from USA *"Do you play ping pong?"*

Yes. But not very often.

Louise, from New Zealand *"Did you mind rubbing noses instead of shaking hands?"*

What people love specially about Diana is the way she fits in. One can't see the Queen or her mother – and certainly not her grandmother – finding it easy to rub noses. But if that's what is expected of *her*, Diana will do it charmingly.

Luke Leach, from Mexico *"What do you do in your spare time?"*

Before Prince William arrived, she loved to swim and dance. But now her favourite spare-time hobby is...playing with her son.

Judy Hu, from China *"Do you like to make pictures like I do?"*

Drawing and painting are not special talents. But when she worked at a nursery school, she loved to watch the children "making pictures".

Chris, 8 from Egypt *"Do you like kissing in public?"*

No. The Royal Family like to keep their farewells and reunions as private as possible. We didn't actually see the Queen saying goodbye to Prince Andrew when he left for the Falklands, or kissing him on his return. Diana probably regrets kissing Prince Charles goodbye in public, the first time he went away after they were engaged, because everyone could see she was crying.

> Dear Princess Diana
> Do you like kissing in public?
> Do you day dream?
> Do you go to sleep in Thermal underwear?
> Do you have toys in The bath Tub?
> Do you grow trees
> Chris age 8.

> Dear Princess Diana
> Do you eat big Mac's?
> Juman Malouf 9 years old
> I come from Lebanon.

Juman Malouf, from Lebanon *"Do you eat Big Mac's?"*

She prefers a fish salad.

Elise, from South Africa *"Why do royal people have so many names?"*

When the Archbishop of Canterbury christened Mary, future wife of George V, he nearly ran out of breath. There were eight names – Victoria Mary Augusta Louise Olga Pauline Claudine Agnes. Afterwards her friends and family simply knew her as May. (She was born in May and her mother referred to her as "my May-flower".) Children of great families didn't *need* all those names. Queen Mary may have forgotten some of her own. But it was a compliment to important friends and relations to say, "I'm calling my child after you." That's why they had so many.

Ali Kawsar, from Bangladesh *"Do you like watching polo?"*

She goes to polo matches and watches her husband play. But she doesn't pretend that this is her favourite sport.

Nicole, from France *"Can you speak a lot of languages?"*

Not one of Diana's best subjects at school. But she did manage to speak some Welsh when she and Prince Charles visited Wales soon after their marriage. More remarkably, she greeted the Aborigines in Australia with a few words in their own language – the Pitjantjatara dialect. They were amazed!

Jacynth, from Colorado *"Would you have your face lifted?"*

The wives of many well-known men would say, "why not?" Betty Ford, wife of an American president, said a face lift made her feel like a million dollars. Most filmstars reckon that if you need it, you ought to have it. Maybe there are members of the Royal Family who would agree.

But the Queen has always said, "I'm not a filmstar." She'd never pretend to be years younger than her real age. She wears practical rather than glamorous spectacles. Face lifts are out.

In matters of fashion and beauty, Diana may not follow in Mother-in-Law's footsteps. We can be pretty sure she'll make up her own mind – *when the time comes*. But that time is still a long way off.

Dear Princess Diana,

Do you dye your hair?

Genna Preston 9

I come from Miami.

> What dose your house look like?
> Love,
> Danielle Ehardt
> age 8

Natasha Forsyth, from Louisiana, USA *"Were you always happy at school?"*

She wasn't happy when her parents were getting divorced and all her schoolfellows could read reports in the newspapers about the case. Who was to blame? Should the children stay with the father or go with the mother? Belonging to a famous family is not all fun; but it was to be good training for her future life as Princess. Even as a young girl she had to learn to live with publicity – with strangers talking about and writing about her private life.

Kevin, from USA *"Do you take showers together?"*

Prince Charles isn't very keen on showers. He prefers a large, old-fashioned bath.

Glen Boss, from USA *"Do you talk to Mrs Thatcher?"*

Yes. They meet up occasionally and will talk – but not about politics. The Princess has been advised to keep away from the subject.

Ashleigh Mace 8

Hilda, from Australia *"Do you ever get the wrong clothes?"*

The fashion experts feel that the blue outfit, chosen for her first engagement pictures, was not a great success. It was safe and sensible – but a bit too matronly for such a young, slim girl. They also think she may have gone to the other extreme when she appeared, soon after, at Goldsmith's Hall. It was her first evening out as the future Princess of Wales; and she wore a black, sequined, strapless dress – *very* low-cut. Rather too revealing, it was said.

Hans, from Germany *"Do you talk to your neighbours?"*

Their country home, Highgrove House, is only a few miles away from the home of Prince Charles's sister and brother-in-law. Kensington Palace, the London home, has been called a royal village. Princess Margaret (Aunt Margo, as they call her), the Duke and Duchess of Gloucester, Prince and Princess Michael of Kent are all close neighbours. The children play together, mothers meet for coffee and a chat, informal dinners are frequent. A friend describes it as "a lovely Happy Families atmosphere". True to say, though, that the royal circle of neighbours is a bit restricted – mostly to other royals or to families like the Duke and Duchess of Beaufort.

Patrick Caudill, from USA *"Have you ever been attacked by the corgis?"*

We don't know for sure but it's possible. The Queen's corgis have a snappy reputation and not even the most popular princess in the world can be absolutely safe.

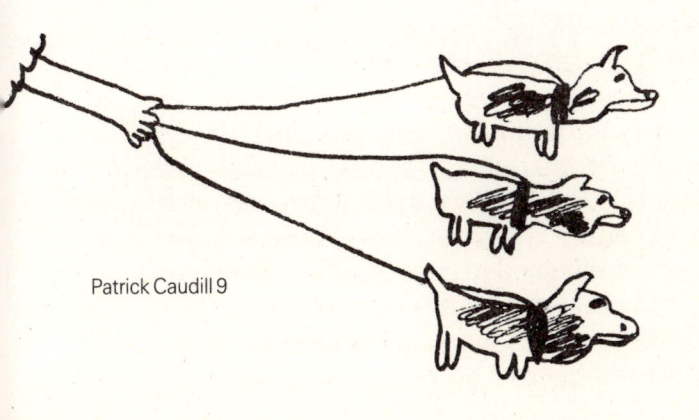

Patrick Caudill 9

5
Dear Other Princesses

The children could, if they chose, address their questions to the Princess of Wales. And that's what most of them did. But they were also asked to think about other princesses. What would they most like to ask *them*?

Diana might be the favourite, but there was plenty of interest in other members of the Royal Family.

Dear Princess Margaret
Mariette, age 9 *"I was sad about you and your husband because my mum and dad were divorced and I know what it's like and I wondered if you minded being on your own?"*

This question, or ones like it, came up very often. No one said: "Why did you get divorced?" or "Isn't it wrong?" Overwhelmingly, there was a sense of sympathy. They seemed to understand that she has been through a difficult, unhappy time – perhaps like their own mothers – and that even a royal princess can be lonely. Princess Margaret is, however, very lucky in her children. They have always been fond of both parents and helped to make the separation easier. Undoubtedly, she would prefer *not* to be on her own. But she has settled down in her new life and is determined to make a success of it.

Dear Princess Alexandra
Lucy, age 11 *"You always look a happy person. Are you?"*

Alexandra's school report from her headmistress once ran: "She has all the lovable qualities of quick sympathy, affection and generosity, laughter and total honesty." She has always been a bit unconventional. Again at school, the matron – scolding the Princess for her untidiness – found herself being hugged with a cry: "Oh darling matron, I'm so sorry!" She is indeed a warm and happy person, and the quality shines through her photographs and public appearances. She's been called "a bit scatty", too. But everyone forgives her.

Dear Princess Michael
Diana, age 9 *"Do you mind being pregnant like my mum does?"*

She's healthy and manages pretty well. But she enjoys social life and official engagements and finds being pregnant a drawback on these occasions. She says that when you're six feet tall and six months gone, it's not easy to plant a tree or launch a submarine or look your best in a beautiful dress.

Dear Princess Margaret
Martin, age 8 *"Were you always fatter than your sister?"*

When George VI and Queen Elizabeth came back from Canada, just before the War, Margaret said to her mother: "Look, Mummie, I am quite a good shape now, not like a football as I used to be!" For she *did* like her sweets, and *did* tend to be pretty round, whereas Elizabeth – much less interested in food – was the slim one.

Dear Princess Anne
"How often do you fall off your horse?"

Very often – like her husband. As a small boy he says he used to count the times, "... it got up to seventy-eight: after that I lost count." And Princess Anne, who was something of a daredevil, never even worried about counting. She would just get back on again.

Antoine Brooks 9

Dear Princess Anne
Joanie, age 8 *"Which is your favourite horse and which is your husband's?"*

Anne had a very special feeling for Doublet, the horse which won the famous European Three-Day Event in 1971. Mark adored a horse called Rock On. (Also known as Sloppy Jo because he was very affectionate and loved people to make a fuss of him.) Mark says he was incredibly proud and brave. "He always had his ears pricked up, saying 'come on, Dad – let's get on with it.' He didn't know what it was to give up." When he died, Mark confesses: "I cried and cried and cried. And even now, just talking about him, gives me a funny feeling."

Dear Princess Caroline of Monaco
Josie, age 10 *"Woud you be more royal if you married someone like Prince Andrew?"*

If you say "Royal Family", chances are people will think of the British Royal Family. If Princess Caroline had married Prince Andrew, she would have joined the best-known Royal Family in the world. But the Queen would probably say that being royal is not a question of being famous; and no, she wouldn't be *more* royal.

Dear Princess Michael
Maxie, age 8 *"Do you like the same animals as the rest of the Royal Family?"*

No. She's very fond of Siamese cats and has four. On the whole, members of the Royal Family are not cat-lovers.

Dear Princess Margaret
Ela, age 7 *"Do you quarrel with your sister and family?"*

They have family rows, Margaret says, "but never feuds".

Dear Princess Anne
Jack, age 12 *"Did you like your school and do you go back there?"*

She was back at her old school, Benenden, quite recently to help celebrate its Diamond Jubilee. It was a December day; but the Princess – even in torrential rain – insisted on going ahead with a tree-planting ceremony. (She chose an English oak.) She talked about "being back home" – perhaps the surest sign that she really had enjoyed her schooldays.

Dear Princess Michael
June, age 10 *"Why do they call you Princess Michael instead of Princess your own name? I don't know what your own name is."*

Her own name is Marie-Christine. And she is called Princess Michael because only the daughters of the Monarch (like Princess Margaret or Princess Anne) or the daughters of a Monarch's son (like Princess Alexandra) are entitled to be called by their own name, following the title "Princess". Strictly speaking, the Princess of Wales should not be called Princess Diana because – like Princess Michael – she is a princess by marriage and not in her own right. But the public decided to think of her as Princess Diana or Princess Di and no one can stop them doing it.

Dear Princess Alexandra
Michael *"Have you done other things as well as being a princess?"*

Yes. She trained as a nurse at the Great Ormond Street Hospital.

Dear Princess Anne
Donna *"Why aren't you the Princess Royal?"*

The title Princess Royal – like the title Prince of Wales – isn't given automatically to the eldest daughter or son of the monarch. It's the gift of the monarch, and it's up to the king or queen to decide if and when it should be given. Quite possibly Princess Anne *will* be made Princess Royal at any time. After all her work for the Save the Children Fund, many people feel she deserves it.

David Craigie 7

Dear Princess Margaret
"Did you ever wish you weren't royal?"

At one time, Princess Margaret said she couldn't imagine anything more wonderful than being a princess. But she has also hankered after an acting or singing career. It's just possible that, if she were now a seventeen-year-old, she could go on the stage. (No one thinks it particularly odd that her son, Viscount Linley, should work as a cabinet-maker.) But it was completely out of the question in her young days. She must have felt at times that being royal meant she couldn't use all her talents. And it meant, of course, that she couldn't marry the man of her choice: Peter Townsend.

Dear Princess Michael
Helen *"What did you do before you were married?"*

She worked as an interior decorator.

Dear Princess Alexandra
Jamie, age 9 *"Would you have liked to be Queen or not?"*

One reason she would say "not" is because of the effect on her husband. As Consort of the Queen, Angus Ogilvy would have had to give up his business career. The happy, relaxed family life they enjoy so much might have suffered if he'd been forced into the life of a full-time royal – instead of being allowed to continue with his own interests. Perhaps, too, Alexandra might feel that her own nature was not suited to the formal job of a reigning Monarch. As said earlier, she is a warm, impulsive person. Strict royal etiquette would not appeal to her for too much of the time.

Dear Princess Anne
Lily *"Do you and Mark quarrel about riding?"*

When they're training together, they've made a rule that they don't criticise each other – not unless one asks advice from the other. Mark says it would be fatal if they started saying to each other: "Sit up! Use your seat a bit more! Left foot back a bit!" Obviously the rule isn't always kept and there are arguments. But Princess Anne says, "Even if you do have a bit of a barney, by the time you get back to the stables, it's either made sense or it hasn't... you've probably translated it into something useful."

Dear Princess Anne
Nick *"Did you enjoy your honeymoon?"*

Not the first four days. They were both seasick on the yacht *Britannia*.

Oliver Davies 6

Dear Princess Anne
Hector, age 9 *"Do you like children as well as horses?"*

When you see her with children, perhaps there isn't the easy, obvious affection that exists between the Princess of Wales and the young, but the love *is* there. Anne spends much time and effort working for Save The Children, and this has included long, gruelling tours in Africa. It's something she cares about very much.

Dear Princess Anne
Tony *"Were you glad to have a boy first?"*

When she started labour on the first baby, Mr Pinker, the gynaecologist, asked if she wanted a boy or girl. Princess Anne said that, as this was the Queen's first grandchild, she supposed it ought to be a boy. But she added that so long as it had ten fingers and ten toes, she didn't really give a hoot.

Robert Youdrell 6

6
Questions We Just Can't Answer

"Do you like the Queen?"
"Who's the most boring person you've met since you became Princess of Wales?"
"Do you think Mrs Thatcher is a good Prime Minister?"
"Do you get on well with Mark Phillips?"
"Do you and Prince Charles sleep in a double bed?"
"Did you like Australia better than New Zealand?"
"Do you think the Queen should abdicate before Charles gets too old?"
"Do you cut your own toenails?"
"Do you think Prince Philip was a bad father?"
"Which party would you vote for at the next election?"

DEAR PRINCESS DIANA,
DOES WILLIAM EVER PICK HIS NOSE?
                    JERRY DORR,
                    AGE 9

There are a lot of things the Royal Family can't talk about. Imagine the headlines, world-wide, if the Princess of Wales said she was bored stiff by President Mitterand or the King of Saudi Arabia, if she thought

> Dear Princess Diana,
> What is your best month?
> Why? Do you like dogs?
> bark bark
>
> Anis Akbar
> Age 8

it was high time the Queen went into retirement, that no one in their senses would vote Labour, that Princess Margaret wore too much make-up, and that she never wanted to visit Norway again.

There's also the feeling: "I must keep *some* of my life private." Small details about her home and habits may seem unimportant, but when you spend so much time in public, with journalists and photographers in hot pursuit, the time comes when you want to shut the door and say, "That's enough."

Children understand this. Perhaps the feeling was best summed up by a little girl from Oxford who sent in six pages of questions, but wrote at the end, "There are so many things I want to know about the Princess but it probably gets boring for her so please tell her not to worry. I'll go on loving her anyway."

Laura Millerleile 8